To Jeanie,

Thinking of you.
Hope you get better
very soon.

Love from
Nicki xx.

Ten Poems
of Light

ex libris

Candlestick Press

Published by:
Candlestick Press,
Diversity House, 72 Nottingham Road, Arnold, Nottingham NG5 6LF
www.candlestickpress.co.uk

Design and typesetting by Craig Twigg

Printed by Bayliss Printing Company Ltd of Worksop, UK

Introduction © Di Slaney, 2024

Cover illustration © Rebecca Vincent, 2024
https://www.rebecca-vincent.co.uk/

Candlestick Press monogram © Barbara Shaw, 2008

© Candlestick Press, 2024

Donation to Starlight Children's Foundation
https://www.starlight.org.uk/

ISBN 978 1 913627 47 8

Acknowledgements

All poems first published in this pamphlet by kind permission of the authors.

Contents

Page

Introduction

Shine a light, keep the light on, light at the end of the tunnel…
we have so many sayings where illumination lifts us up and
keeps us going. For Candlestick Press the opportunity to
celebrate shining a light for poetry with the sale of our millionth
pamphlet was too good to miss, and so *Ten Poems about Light*
has been published to mark this significant milestone.

We've been delighted to include ten brand new poems by ten
brilliant poets, nine of whom were winners in our competition
to find different expressions and experiences of light. From the
fox of the Northern Lights to fungal bioluminescence, the silvery
glitter of the sea, a vast hunger for sunlight and a tree that acts as
a radiant conduit, the poets skilfully create worlds of light with
their words.

Of course religious connotations of light can't be ignored,
and Rosie Jackson gives us Magdalene staring at a flame for
transcendence, while commissioned poet Carole Bromley
remembers a loved one with the symbolic acts of prayer and
lighting a candle in a rebuilt cathedral.

We also look at the bigger picture beyond ourselves, as Jane
Burn presents the vast science of light in a moving conversation
with her child, the light of her life. And the pamphlet ends with
Shasta Hanif Ali's lyric list of 'Things that hold light' as a way
to help process grief through tiny glimpses of joy.

We're proud to bring you these wonderful poems for the first
time. Thank you for helping to keep the Candlesticks alight
and aloft in the UK and beyond. Here's to many more beautiful
poems being shared in the world – may the light of poetry never
go out!

Di Slaney

craving

What her friends don't know
when she says
she craves the sunlight

is that she means it literally
secretly she is a tree and
they are light-eaters

as she is starving
through this darkening season
all she can think about is her hunger for it:

bright rays heaped on a china plate
she wants to devour an entire wheel of orange sun
she wants to drink a lake of golden california light

she needs light for all
that is dying inside her
to break into bud

Laura Theis

Telling My Child About Light

Light, I tell you, comes from the sun. I think it takes
only eight minutes to reach us, all the way down here,
ninety-three million miles away. Nothing is faster
than the speed of light, which is why I can see the smile
on your face at the exact time you smiled it. Moonlight
is reflected glow, because the other side of the moon
is always facing the sun – wherever you are in the world,
somewhere there is light. It is only dark for a while –
unless you are very, very far away in the frozen north,
where a polar night can last for thirty days or more.
The Northern Lights mean the sky has truly come alive.
Stars are burning, and Sirius burns the brightest of all.
Light is electromagnetic radiation. Light is waves, shaped
a little like the way you might draw the sea. Light is made
from a rainbow. A rainbow is raindrops scattering light.
Light is energy. Did you know, you can power a lightbulb
by bike? Though you might have to pedal for quite a while.
We cannot see infrared, but it beams between the remote
and the channels on the TV. Flowers use ultraviolet light
to guide the bees – the colours are like maps to the sweet.
Some creatures on Earth have DIY light. Down in the depths,
anglerfish dangle wands of it from their heads. Fireflies
carry lanterns of their own. Algae floats in skins of light.
Those leaves are photosynthesising. A bit like having light
for lunch. Is light flavoured green? Nematodes don't have eyes,
so they taste the light instead. X-rays are a special sort of light
that can see right through to your bones. Light is Christmas,
sparkling round the tree. Light is Diwali, its triumph over dark.
Light is how I can read you to sleep, and you are the light
of my life. Light is the flaming crown of a birthday cake.
When you blow out the candles, where does light go?
It turns into hope. If you want, we can strike a match,
relight each wick and wish all over again.

Jane Burn

Fire lit up the sky

for Kathryn

I slept through it all, sirens, engines,
130 firefighters, timbers crashing to the floor,
molten lead raining down from the roof.
Those who lived nearby told of flames
leaping thirty feet into the sky. By dawn,
when I woke to a smell of burning,
the Rose Window was saved, although
crazed with 40,000 cracks, the fire contained,
that all night sent clergy running in and out
with textiles, furniture, candlesticks.

Forty years have gone by and today
light streams in through the restored glass,
visitors crane their necks to see
the Blue Peter roof bosses: Famine in Africa,
The Moon Landing, Marine Conservation,
The Rose Window in flames, The Mary Rose,
The Conquest of Space. *Light a Candle,*
a sign says, *and say a prayer*, so I do.
I light it for you, you who made the world
a brighter place, and leave it burning.

Carole Bromley

On Monday July 9th, 1984, fire erupted in York Minster's South Transept after
it was struck by lightning.

Magdalene and the Flame

(from Georges de la Tour)

She's staring at the light as if to imprint it
on her retina. Her skirt is the scarlet
of chilli peppers. Someone has put
a polished skull in her lap to pull her
away from her body – it hasn't worked.
Her throat is flushed with warmth,
she seems to have drunk the flame.
The pulse of the blood in her neck
mirrors the candle's flicker. The flame
rises like a wing beating against the night --
she watches it burn and burn and not
diminish. A halo hangs over the table.
She's never sat so still, never leaned
so willingly towards her edges.
Never looked at light this way before –
how it lifts things out of time, quickens them
with the memory of where they come from.
Once, her world was dust, stones, falling.
Now, when she moves closer, her mouth
almost kissing the heat, her breath
sends shadows skittering along the wall,
as if what she sees is her own dream
of book, glass, rope.
Even when she blows out the flame,
it remains alive inside her.
And when dawn arrives, the slow-to-awaken
sky is somehow part of the same insurgency –
birds, clouds, sea, trees, arid hills,
all hauled out of sleep and delivered
back to themselves – sailing upwards
into whatever this one light is.

Rosie Jackson

Flametree

Skara, Sweden 2023

Everyone has passed this tree in time
it grows where autumn is and dark
it is an opera house on fire
in the night when pigeon-breasted cloud
allows a wire of light to earth
Celebrate! it says Or you are nothing.

Stephen Keeler

Desire Lines

The light has got some curves
back on her so now it's been a year,
almost, since I leaned against
the oven and sobbed into ugly
slabs of bread. The bread for dinner,
the dinner burned and while she
saw-tooth screamed against my chest
I stood in rounded light and wished

myself gone. Later I thought
of desire lines, those little forest trails
made by feet when the given path looks
too far to go. That's how it is with us, always wanting

easier ways to be. Whatever wants I had
back then were too unformed to hold, but now
I see those little paths all over,
the earth threaded over with our small
desires. And mine. It's not quite time but

it's spring and in its new-made swagger
light rests on me like a mantle, and when
I say *I want*, the light says *darling,
you can have it.*

Rachel Jeffcoat

Sea-light

We're here to harvest — ahead of inland winter
with its cloudy wrap of darkness — and carry home
as much doubled light as a heart can hold.

> Silvery mornings,
> sky polished to pearl
> and the sea
> a reflective mirror of silk.

We come, eyes sparkling, eager for the flash
in splintering water, to catch the gleam
of dizzying light in crystal sand.

> Whiteness and spray,
> waves rushing sunlight
> across shingle,
> playing *see-me, catch-me, can't.*

We breathe in all the brilliance, hands salted, the sun
stacked in the barns of memory: *look!*
our store of summer radiance, safely gathered in.

DA Prince

Fire Fox

In Finnish legend, the Fire Fox creates the Northern Lights.

He canters on the snow with silent paws,
head down, brush twitching, waiting

for this moment, when hunters pause,
turning North, when cruise ship watchers

grip the rails, because
for a heartbeat's length,

clouds relax, a frost-knife
shaves the air, the planet holds

its breath. He conjures ancient laws,
flicks his tail to whisk up snowflakes,

shreds them in the air with glowing claws,
ignites them with his sparking tail;

green fire flounces in the sky, throbs
light and dark, hemmed with pink and red,

dies down. He dusts his tail, ignores applause,
slinks off towards the point where sky lies down

with snow, where shadows hide,
dissolves in an eternity of white.

Nairn Kennedy

Foxfire

The bioluminescence from a fungus that grows on rotting wood.

I bathe my skin in your cold afterburn,
inferno of moving light. I feel a reckoning
with this rotting wood, each year of me
closer to a world of smelt, orange smoulder,
firestorm under oak and ash.

What a surprise to find your firebolt,
your glow in the dank forest, where mulch
is a world sinking into earth. How you
arouse, excite, tinder today's lethargy.

I thought some kind of unearthly magic afoot;
but here you are,
owl-light,
photo-flood in my eyes,
moonlight pool
of coming to terms with my own tragedy,
mirror of green fire-shine.

Here, my bones are old. Here, my flesh sags,
and here, my heart muscle moans to the music
of loss; but you blaze within the dying of another,
a torch, candle,
pyre of excitement,
swarm of fireflies,
firehouse of promise,
angelic light at the end of the tunnel,
electric arc to heaven.

Penny Sharman

Things that hold light

The way the trees shelter grief at the hospice. Bubbles. Laying in bed listening to the rain beat against your window. When he makes you chai in your favourite mug. Snowdrops bursting through a thawing ground. Another dawn break at the hospice. Petrichor. A sky full of clouds. When one grandmother's name was noor نور meaning light, and the other was jaan جان meaning life. Road trips which were dreams when you were unwell. Books. When you search *what are large daisies called*—discover they're oxeye daisies, and the even larger version are *shasta daisies*. Learning the names of wildflowers. At the hospice, when you truly understand the meaning of *sabr*, as you hold your newborn's tiny fingers in your father's weathered hands. A sky holding a forewarned storm. A blank page in a new notebook. Each child's firsts. The relief after pain. *Shukar*. Languages—though there's never enough words for grief. Summer breeze (even if you can't say this without the song in your head). How you know you've grown, when a poem hits differently each time you read it. Pasta. Crunching leaves beneath your feet. Each breath you hear sitting in the hospice, even if the breath is a steady, beep, beep, beeping, machine. How *roshni* also means light. A cloudless sky. A thick blanket of freshly fallen snow. Birdsong. When we fall, we are gathered. Your children planting flowers at their grandfather's grave. Soil holding memories. Buried seeds turning into seedlings. The wide arms of the future.

Shasta Hanif Ali